EASIEST KEYBOARD COU

by Christopher Hussey

Illustrations by Sergio Sandoval

PLAYBACK+
Speed • Pitch • Balance • Loop

To access audio, visit:
www.halleonard.com/mylibrary

Enter Code
3994-7934-1687-6546

ISBN 978-1-5400-4683-3

WILLIS MUSIC

EXCLUSIVELY DISTRIBUTED BY

HAL•LEONARD®

Visit Hal Leonard Online at
www.halleonard.com

Contact us:
Hal Leonard
7777 West Bluemound Road
Milwaukee, WI 53213
Email: info@halleonard.com

In Europe, contact:
Hal Leonard Europe Limited
42 Wigmore Street
Marylebone, London, W1U 2RN
Email: info@halleonardeurope.com

In Australia, contact:
Hal Leonard Australia Pty. Ltd.
4 Lentara Court
Cheltenham, Victoria, 3192 Australia
Email: info@halleonard.com.au

Teachers and Parents

Purpose

This book is designed to be a flexible resource that brings joy to beginner keyboard students while they learn to read music and develop performance skills. It can be used for both one-on-one and group lessons.

It can be taught from start to finish or used as a resource for activities and performance pieces.

Scope

New notes and new concepts are introduced gradually. By the end, the student will have encountered eighth-note rhythms, dotted quarter notes, and the keys of C, F, and G Major. They will also have played triads with each hand.

Chord symbols are used in the book where they reinforce what is being taught, and avoided where they might cause confusion. Dynamic markings are introduced towards the end, for students with touch-sensitive instruments.

Accompaniments and Audio

Audio tracks, performed both with and without the student part, can be downloaded for all songs – see the inside front cover for details.

The accompaniments in this book may be transposed to any octave to suit the teacher's needs. If the teacher is accompanying on the student's instrument, the instructions in the preface to each piece and the transpositions indicated by the clef or markings underneath the staff will ensure that there is no clashing of hands. Look out for the "octave" bass clef: $\mathbf{9}\!:_{\!s}$, which indicates that the whole staff should be played an octave lower.

Speeds and Voicing

The audio tracks indicate the author's suggested speed and voicing for each piece, but the author would like to encourage the teacher and student to tackle each piece at a tempo that works for them, and to experiment freely with the voices on their instrument. Metronome markings are used occasionally, to indicate the *feel* of a piece.

Contents

Your Keyboard

Try This

Say the letter names of the musical alphabet a few times.

Your keyboard has WHITE KEYS and BLACK KEYS.

The WHITE KEYS are named **A B C D E F G**

Can you see any repeating patterns on your keyboard?

The BLACK KEYS are arranged in groups of TWO and THREE.

Can you press down each of the groups of two black keys on your keyboard?

Finding the note C

The note C is found directly to the left of the group of two black keys.

Write the letter C on all the Cs you can find on the keyboard diagram below.

Now play each of the Cs on your keyboard using your RIGHT-HAND thumb.

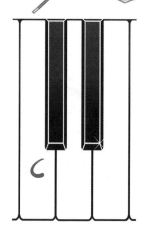

Middle C

The C found near the middle of your keyboard is called MIDDLE C.

Try playing the rhythm of your name on Middle C, using your LEFT-HAND thumb.

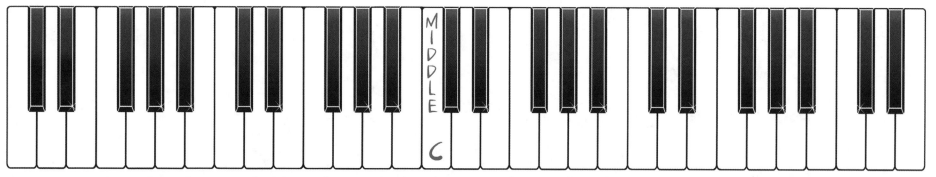

As you learn the name of each new key, turn back to this page and write its letter name on ALL the keys with that name.

The Staff and Reading Music

Music is written on five horizontal lines called a STAFF.

NOTES are written on the LINES and in the SPACES of the staff and tell us which KEYS to play.
The music is divided by BAR LINES into MEASURES (also called "bars").

The TIME SIGNATURE at the beginning of the music tells us how to count. The top number tells us how many counts there are in each measure.

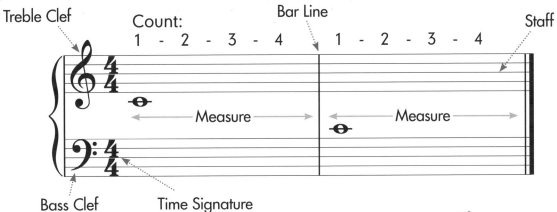

Clefs

This is how you write MIDDLE C in the TREBLE CLEF:

Play notes in the Treble Clef with your RIGHT HAND.

This is how you write Middle C in the BASS CLEF:

Play notes in the Bass Clef with your LEFT HAND.

Finger numbers

The fingers in each hand are numbered from 1 to 5, with both thumbs numbered 1.

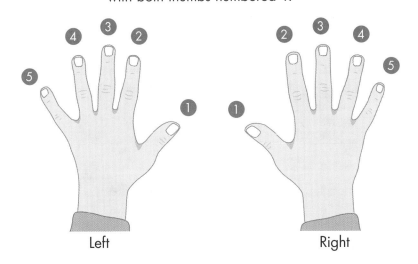

Left   Right

Middle C in the Right Hand

Whole Note

A WHOLE NOTE looks like this: 𝅝

It is held for FOUR COUNTS.

Position your RIGHT HAND with your thumb (finger 1) on MIDDLE C.

Play Middle C many times, holding each as a whole note (four counts).

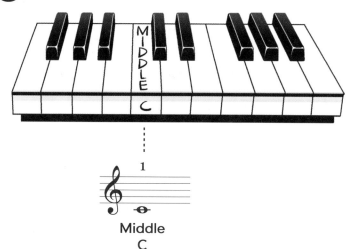

Middle
C

Practice writing whole notes as Middle C in the TREBLE CLEF.
The first one has been done for you.

1/2

Jumping Popcorn!

Count: 1 - 2 - 3 - 4   1 - 2 - 3 - 4   1 - 2 - 3 - 4   1 - 2 - 3 - 4

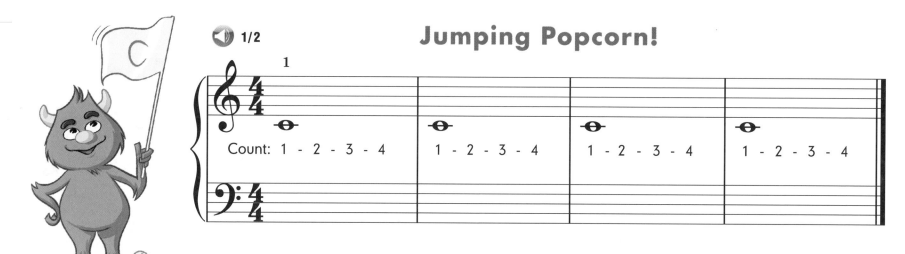

Accompaniment

Middle C in the Left Hand

Half Note

A HALF NOTE looks like this ♩ or ♩.

It is held for TWO COUNTS.

Position your LEFT HAND with your thumb (finger 1) on Middle C.

Play Middle C many times, holding each as a half note (two counts).

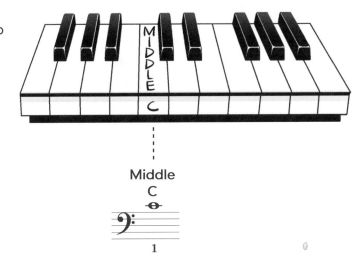

Middle
C

Practice writing half notes on the note Middle C in the BASS CLEF.

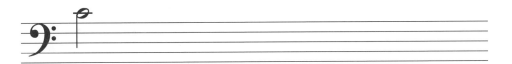

3/4 Deep Beneath the Ocean's Floor

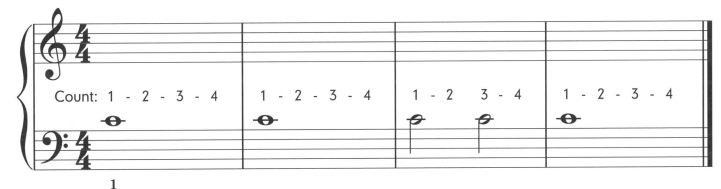

Count: 1 - 2 - 3 - 4   1 - 2 - 3 - 4   1 - 2   3 - 4   1 - 2 - 3 - 4

Accompaniment

New Note: D

Dance, Dance, Dance to the Beat

5/6

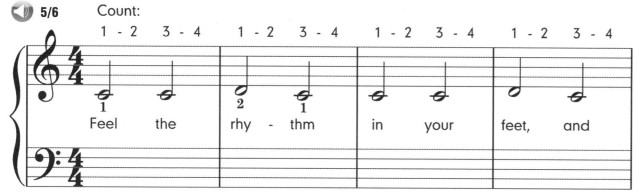

Count:
1 - 2   3 - 4   1 - 2   3 - 4   1 - 2   3 - 4   1 - 2   3 - 4

Feel   the   rhy - thm   in   your   feet,   and

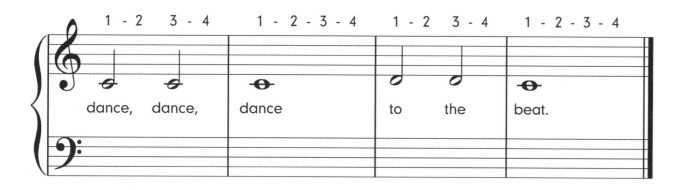

1 - 2   3 - 4   1 - 2 - 3 - 4   1 - 2   3 - 4   1 - 2 - 3 - 4

dance, dance,   dance   to   the   beat.

RIGHT HAND

1   2

Middle   D
C

Try This

Set your keyboard tempo to 96 beats per minute and choose a drum beat, e.g. Rock or Disco, to play along with.

Accompaniment

Quarter Note

A QUARTER NOTE looks like this ♩ or ♪ .
It is held for ONE COUNT.

New Note: B

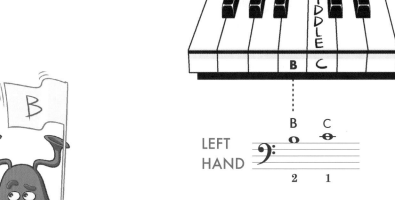

B **C**

LEFT
HAND

B C

2 1

Painted Sky

7/8

Count:
1 - 2   3 - 4   1 - 2 - 3 - 4

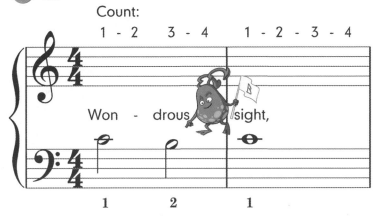

Won - drous sight,

1   2   1

Try This

Choose a Strings voice on
your keyboard for this song.

1 - 2   3 - 4 | 1 - 2 - 3 - 4 | 1   2   3   4 | 1 - 2   3 - 4 | 1   2   3   4 | 1 - 2 - 3 - 4

col - ors | bright. | Just be - fore the | twi - light | glows the paint - ed | sky.

Accompaniment

Musical Crossword

Across

1 This note ♩ gets ONE COUNT and is called a _ _ _ _ _ _ _ note.

2 Notes played by your LEFT HAND are written in the _ _ _ _ clef.

3 **3/4** tells us there are how many counts to each measure? _ _ _ _ _.

4 _ _ _ _ _ _ _ is the name of the note that is found to the left of the TWO BLACK KEYS near the center of your keyboard.

Down

1 Music is divided by _ _ _ lines into groups containing an equal number of counts.

2 This note ♩ gets TWO COUNTS and is called a _ _ _ _ note.

3 Notes played by your RIGHT HAND are written in the _ _ _ _ _ _ clef.

4 Music is written on five horizontal lines, called a _ _ _ _ _ .

5 This note 𝅝 gets FOUR COUNTS and is called a _ _ _ _ _ note.

Writing Challenge

Fill measure 1 with QUARTER NOTES on D and measure 2 with quarter notes on MIDDLE C.

Fill measure 1 with HALF NOTES on Middle C and measure 2 with half notes on B.

Can you play the music you've written above on your keyboard?

Counting in Two and New Note: E

Time signature

$\frac{2}{4}$ ("Two-four") tells you to count TWO in each measure.

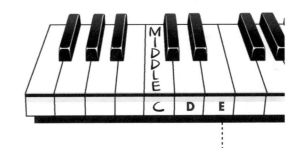

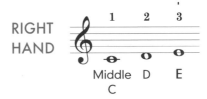

RIGHT HAND

Middle C   D   E

Sleepy Hedgehog

9/10

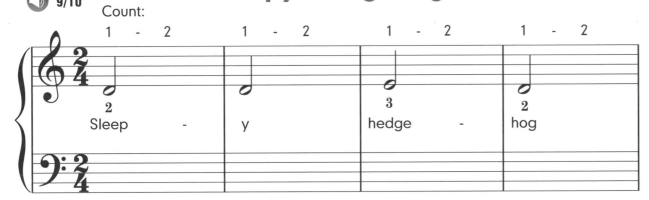

Count:
1 - 2   1 - 2   1 - 2   1 - 2

Sleep - y   hedge - hog

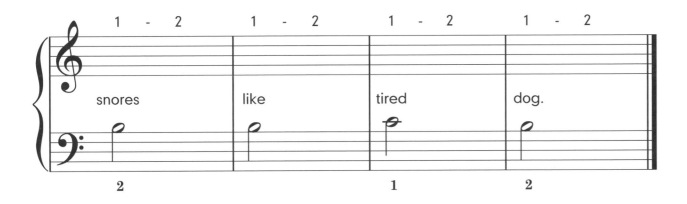

1 - 2   1 - 2   1 - 2   1 - 2

snores   like   tired   dog.

Note Practice

Accompaniment

Swung

Counting in Three and New Note: A

Time signature

¾ ("Three-four") tells you to count THREE in each measure.

Dotted Half Note

A DOTTED HALF NOTE looks like this 𝅗𝅥. or ♩. It is held for THREE COUNTS.

🔊 **11/12**

Jolly Romilly, the Pirate Queen

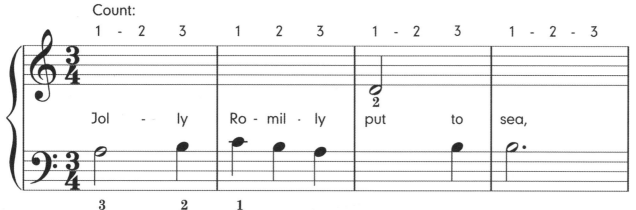

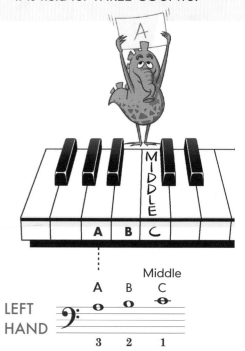

Note Practice

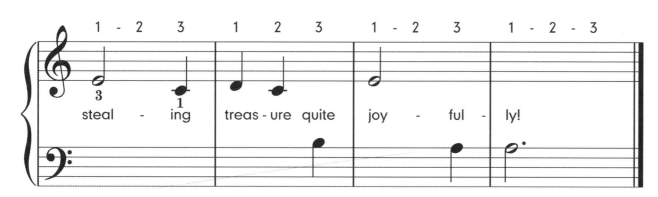

Accompaniment

Repeat Sign and
New Note: F

Jousting Knights

13/14

repeat sign

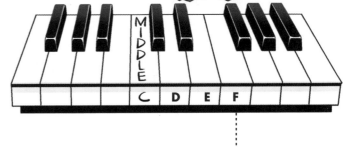

RIGHT HAND

Middle C · D · E · F

Repeat sign :‖

This sign tells you to go back to the beginning and play the tune again.

Accompaniment

New Note: G

Candlelight Boogie

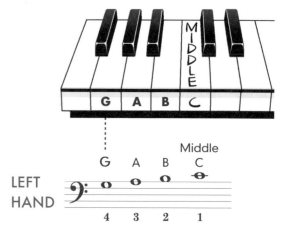

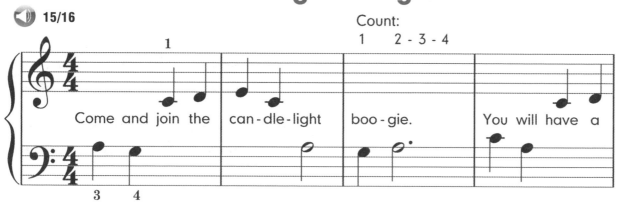

Accompaniment

New Note: G

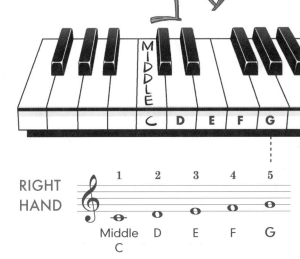

The Kangaroo from Timbuktu

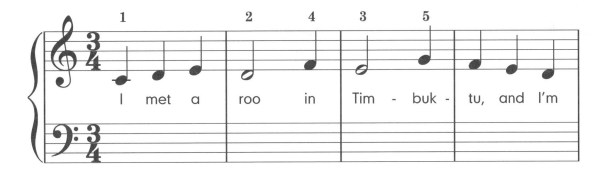

I met a roo in Tim - buk - tu, and I'm

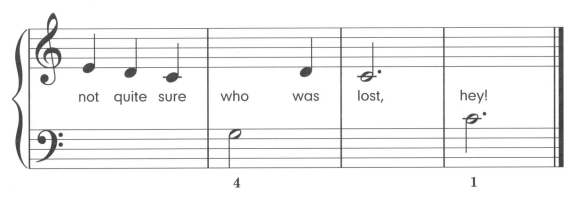

not quite sure who was lost, hey!

Note Practice

Accompaniment

Swung

Rests and Counting

RESTS in the music tell you to be silent — each note value has a rest indicating a silence for the same number of counts.

Whole rest

Be silent for
FOUR COUNTS or a WHOLE
MEASURE in any time signature

Half rest

Be silent for
TWO COUNTS

Quarter rest

Be silent for
ONE COUNT

Missing Bar Lines Puzzle

In the following examples, draw the missing bar lines so that each measure
contains the right number of counts as shown in the time signature.

Count the time values of the notes and rests carefully! When you've finished, try playing the tunes.

Try This

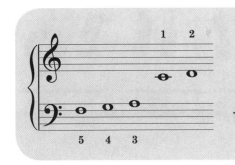

Improvise your own tune to fit with the accompaniment using only these five notes.

This group of notes is called the PENTATONIC SCALE.

New Note: F

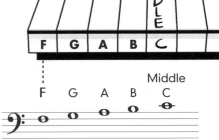

LEFT HAND

🔊 **19/20**

Fairy-Fly

Accompaniment

♩ = 80

With pedal (if possible)

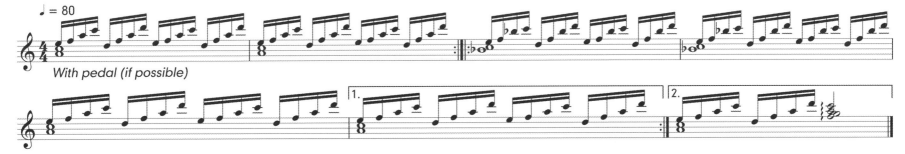

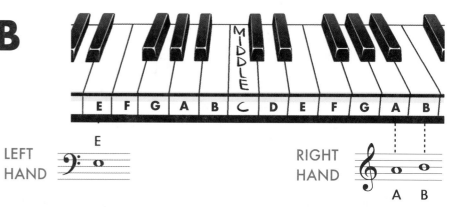

New Notes: E, A, and B

Play these notes

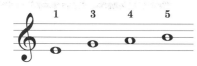

Name
them: ___ ___ ___ ___

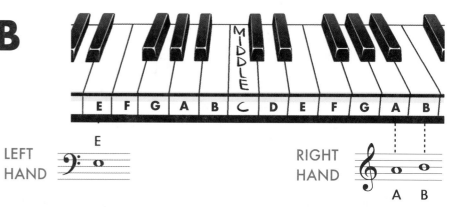

Try This

Once you've learned this melody, using only these four notes, improvise your own melody to fit the accompaniment.

LEFT HAND
E

RIGHT HAND
A B

Look at the finger numbers to work out the new positions for your hands. Choose a Jazz Organ or Electric Piano voice on your keyboard.

🔊 21/22

Tuesday Blues

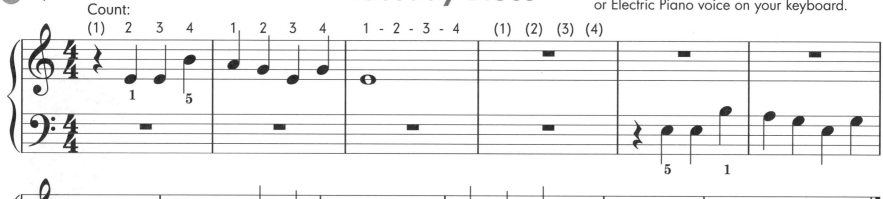

Accompaniment

When performed with accompaniment, the student's part should be played up an octave.

New Note: D and Ties

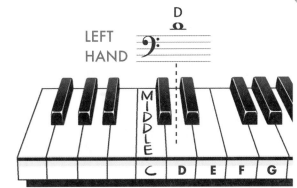

LEFT HAND — D

The Tie

A TIE is a curved line that joins two notes of the same pitch.

Only the first note is played, and it is held for the length of both tied notes.

23/24

Crocodile's Stomp

Count:
1 - 2 - 3   4 -   1   2   3   4   1 - 2   3   4 -   1 - 2 - 3 - 4

repeat from here

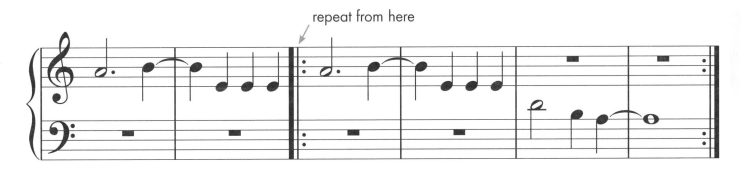

Look carefully at the finger numbers for each hand before you play, to work out their new positions.

Accompaniment

sim.

Eighth Notes

A pair of EIGHTH NOTES looks like this: ♫ or ♫

There are two eighth notes to ONE COUNT.

Try This

Count:
1 and 2 and 3 and 4 and 1 and 2 and 3 - 4

Play this finger warm-up in your RIGHT HAND.

Then try it an OCTAVE lower in your LEFT HAND, starting on the next E down your keyboard to the left. Position finger 4 of your left hand on this E to begin.

Have You Ever Seen an Octopus Play the Bagpipes?

Position both your thumbs on the D to the right of MIDDLE C to play this song.

25/26

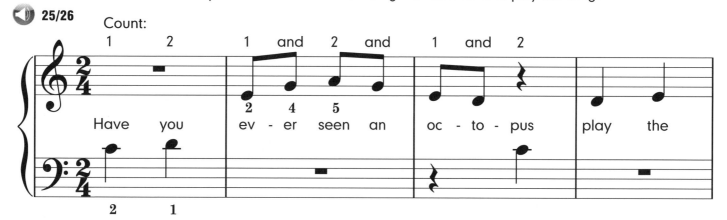

Count:
1   2   1 and 2 and   1 and 2

Have you   ev - er seen an   oc - to - pus   play the

Accompaniment

New Notes: C and D

Try This

Experiment with different voices on your keyboard and choose one that you like the best. Try a Bell or Choir voice, or Strings.

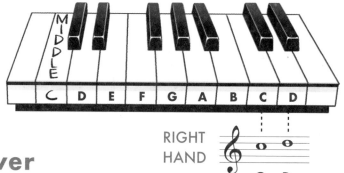

Princess in the Tower

27/28

Look at the finger numbers to work out where to position your hands.

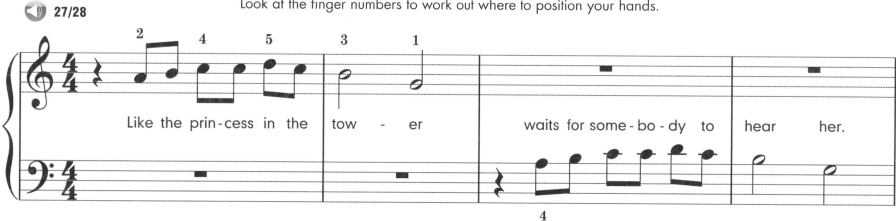

Like the prin-cess in the tow - er   waits for some-bo-dy to   hear her.

Sing - ing sweet - ly;   when some - one comes,   she'll let down her   hair.

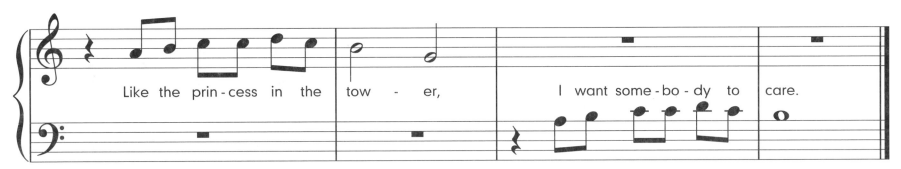

Like the prin - cess in the tow - er, I want some - bo - dy to care.

Try This

Keep the same hand positions. Using your RIGHT HAND only, try improvising your own melody to fit with the accompaniment using the five notes from G up to D.

Then try improvising a melody with your LEFT HAND.

Accompaniment

New Notes and Hands Together

Position your RIGHT-HAND thumb on MIDDLE C and your LEFT-HAND finger 5 on the C an OCTAVE below (the next C down your keyboard to the left).

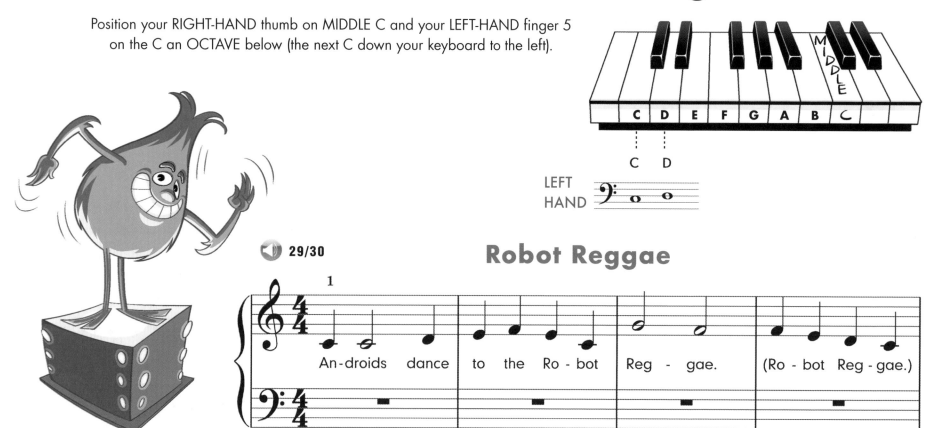

29/30

Robot Reggae

An-droids dance | to the Ro-bot | Reg - gae. | (Ro - bot Reg - gae.)

Mov - ing un - | til their met - al | legs ache. | (Met - al legs ache.)

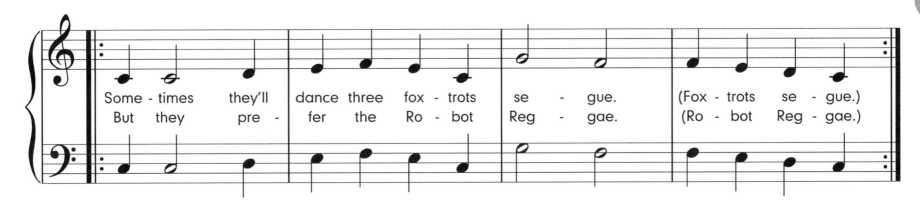

Some - times   they'll   dance three   fox - trots   se -   gue.   (Fox - trots   se - gue.)
But   they   pre -   fer   the   Ro - bot   Reg -   gae.   (Ro - bot   Reg - gae.)

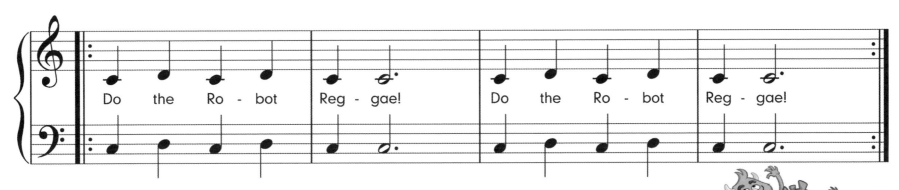

Do   the   Ro - bot   Reg - gae!   Do   the   Ro - bot   Reg - gae!

Accompaniment

Play left hand only with the student's part. When the song is learned, the student's part should be played up an octave and the right hand of the accompaniment can be added.

Reggae shuffle

8vb

(8)

My Secret Flying Machine

Try This

Experiment with different voices on your keyboard.

Which sound do you think works best?

My se - cret fly - ing mach - ine

takes off each night. I'm all set for ad -

ven - ture. Speed: fast - er than light! _____

Accompaniment

When performed with accompaniment, the student's part should be played up an octave.

With pedal (if possible)

Eighth Note with Dotted Quarter Note

Try playing the following rhythms on any note you choose, counting carefully as you play.

Count:
1 - 2 and 3   4

Count:
1 - 2 and - 3   4

New rhythms

An eighth note ♪ or ♫ lasts HALF A COUNT.

A dotted quarter note ♩. or ♩ lasts ONE-AND-A-HALF COUNTS.

Moon Rabbit

🔊 33/34

Position your hands with both thumbs on MIDDLE C.
Why not make up some words to fit the RIGHT-HAND melody?

Count:
1 - 2 and 3   4   1 - 2 and 3 - 4

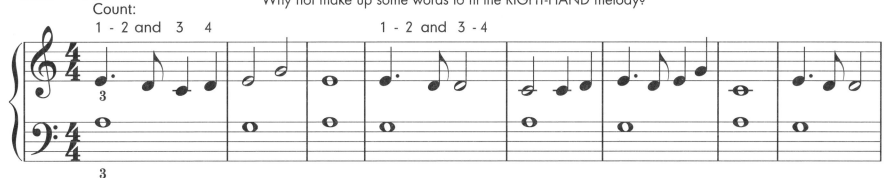

1 - 2 and - 3   4

Accompaniment

light staccato   **Play 3 times**

Note-Spelling

Write in the letter names to reveal the word that each tune spells! Then try playing each one on the keyboard.

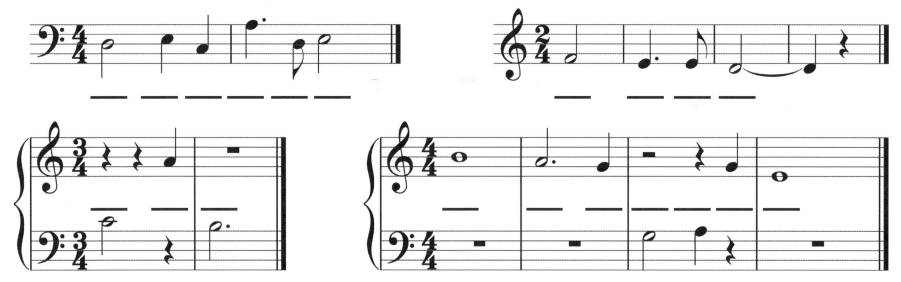

In the empty measures below, draw the note for each letter under the staff. The note value is shown above.
Then play the tune that each word makes.

F A C E

B A D G E

C A B B A G E

The Sharp Sign and F♯

When a SHARP (♯) is placed before a note, it raises the note a half step to the very next key on the RIGHT.

F-SHARP (F♯) is the BLACK KEY just to the right of F.

How many can you find on your keyboard?

This song begins on the second count of the measure.

There is only one count in the last measure to balance.

New positions for your hands

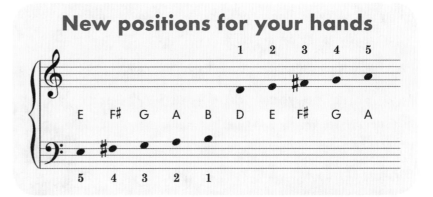

🔊 35/36

The Gnome's Magic Spell

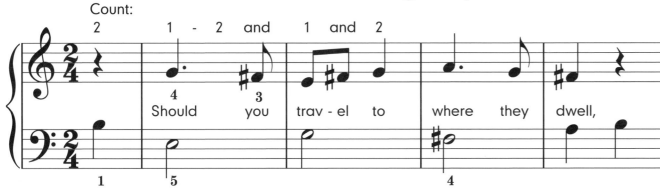

Count:
2   1 - 2 and   1 and 2

Should you   trav-el to   where they dwell,

you'll come   un - der the   gnome's mag - ic   spell.

Try This

Play the notes above as half notes, then quarter notes, then eighth notes.

Accompaniment

The Flat Sign and B♭

When a FLAT (♭) is placed before a note, it lowers the note a half step to the very next key on the LEFT.

B-FLAT (B♭) is the BLACK KEY just to the left of B.

How many can you find on your keyboard?

New positions for your hands

🔊 37/38

Big Top Tomfoolery

Big top tom-fool-er-y, pails of wa-ter are top - pling!

Big Top tom-fool-er-y, clown-ing all round the ring.

Accompaniment

Try This

Play this rhythm on any note you choose, counting carefully as you play.

Count:
1   and - 2   and   3   4

King of   sa - fa - ri

King of Safari

39/40

Accompaniment

Chords: C, F, and G Major Triads

Triads

When two or more notes are played together, they form a CHORD.

The most common type of chord is a three-note chord. These are called TRIADS.

Practice playing the three triads below in your RIGHT HAND, holding each chord for FOUR COUNTS.

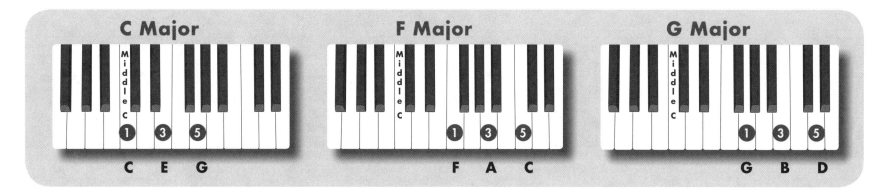

Name the Chords

Play the right-hand chord sequences below a few times each. Can you name the chords you are playing?

Can you make up some words for the rhythm of each of them?

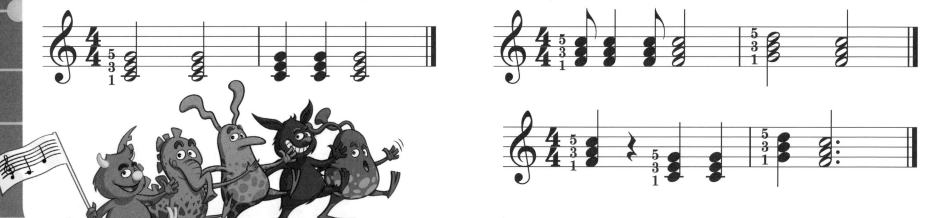

Do you recognize the chords used in measure 1?

41/42

On the Trampoline!

Try This

Choose a Synth voice on your keyboard.

Set your keyboard tempo to 76 beats per minute. Can you find a drum beat that works well?

Accompaniment

When performed with accompaniment, the student's part should be played up an octave.

Key Signature: F Major

When the FLAT or SHARP sign appears just after the clef, it is called a KEY SIGNATURE.

The key signature below tells us that all the Bs are played as B-flats — in the RIGHT HAND and the LEFT HAND. This is the key signature of F MAJOR.

Practice playing these chords with your RIGHT HAND only, then LEFT HAND only, and finally, hands together.

F Major   F suspended fourth

Dragon in the Clouds

43/44

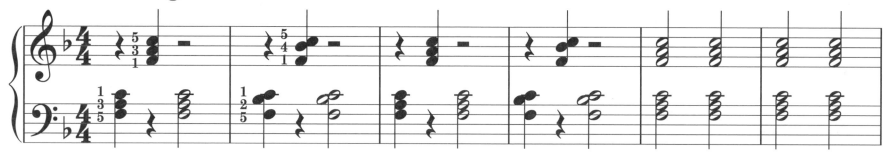

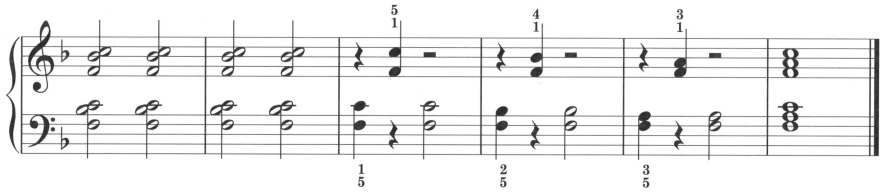

Accompaniment

When performed with accompaniment, the student's part should be played up an octave.

Key Signature: G Major

In this piece, the key signature tells us that all the Fs are played as F-sharps — in both hands. This is the key signature of G MAJOR.

Practice these chords in both hands before you play.

In this piece, instead of playing the notes together as triads, they are sounded separately as BROKEN CHORDS.

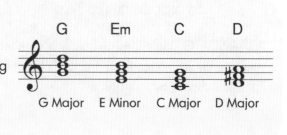

G	Em	C	D
G Major	E Minor	C Major	D Major

🔊 45/46

Operation Space Station

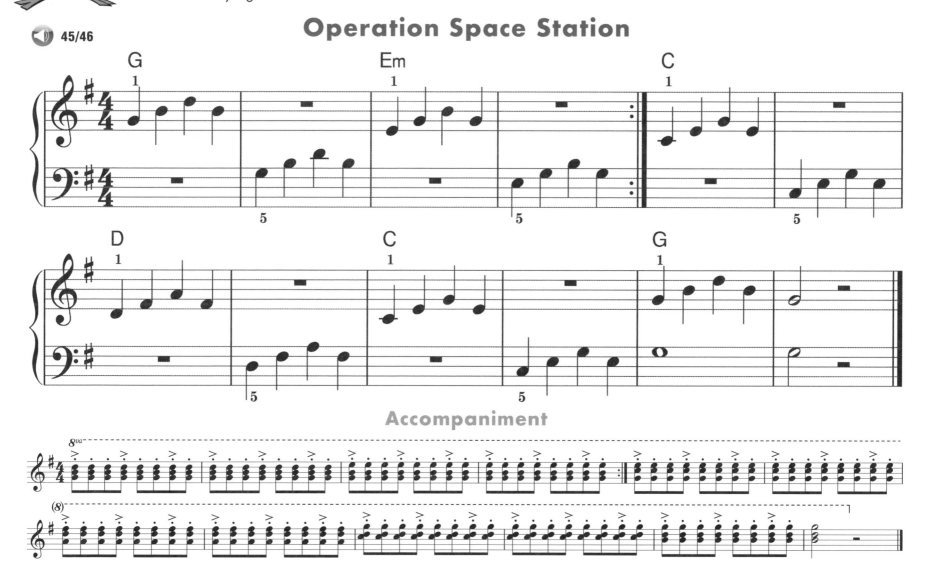

Accompaniment

Staccato notes

A STACCATO dot above or below a note tells you to play it shorter than written. Play them lightly and with a bounce.

It's Time to Party!

Can you spot the TRIADS of G Major, E Minor, and C Major that you've already learned?
Watch out for the C Major triad over a D bass note in the LEFT HAND in measures 7 and 8.

47/48

Count:
1 - 2 and - 3 - 4

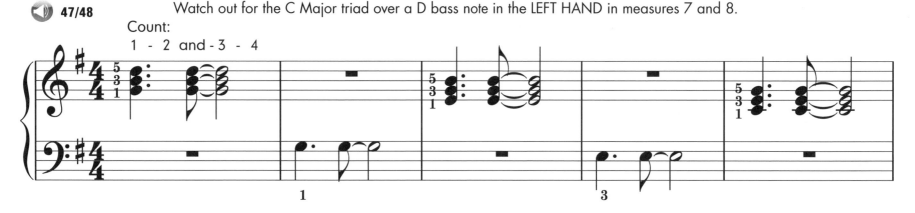

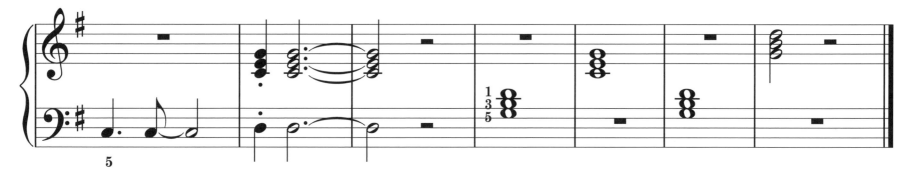

Accompaniment

Odd One Out

Can you spot and draw a circle around the odd one out in each bubble?

Chords

Practice playing these RIGHT-HAND triads.

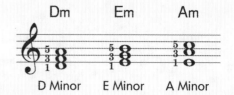

D Minor   E Minor   A Minor

This tune is in a MINOR key and uses all minor chords.

Minor keys are often used to create a sad or reflective tone.
How would you describe this tune?

Kites on Parade

49/50

Accompaniment

Using both hands, play the accompaniment at written pitch in the left hand and up two octaves (or one if not possible) in the right hand.

Practice playing these left-hand chords, holding each for four counts.

Watching the Waves

Learn this simple RIGHT-HAND OSTINATO (a repeating phrase) before adding the left-hand chords.

Choose how many times to repeat the first four measures before continuing to the ending.

51/52

Accompaniment

When performed with accompaniment, the student's part should be played up an octave.

Try This

Set your keyboard tempo to 100 beats per minute and choose a drum beat, e.g. Soft Rock or 8-beat, to play along with.

Try using auto-chords or auto-accompaniment to fill out your left-hand chords. To do this, you will probably have to play the left-hand chords an octave lower, or change the accompaniment split-point on your keyboard.

Dynamics

If your keyboard has touch-sensitive keys, follow the DYNAMIC MARKINGS for the rest of this book.

p stands for PIANO (pronounced "pee-ah-no"), meaning quiet.

f stands for FORTE (pronounced "for-tay"), meaning loud.

Under the Shooting Stars

53/54

Practice the RIGHT HAND on its own to begin with, then the LEFT HAND on its own, before putting them together.

Both hands 8va throughout

Accompaniment

The Natural Sign

When a NATURAL (♮) is placed before a note, it cancels the effect
of a sharp or flat earlier in the bar, in the previous bar, or in the key signature.

In this piece, there is an F-natural after an F-sharp and an
E-natural following an E-flat. Can you find them in the music?

E-FLAT (E♭) is the BLACK
KEY just to the left of E.

**How many can you
find on your keyboard?**

55/56

Rainbow Bouquet

Watch for the shifting hand positions in this piece — follow the fingering carefully. Try using a gospel organ voice for this tune.

Accompaniment

Play the left hand only with the student's part. When the song is learned, the student's part should be
played up an octave and the right hand of the accompaniment can be added.

Match the Pairs

Play through the left-hand chord sequences below a few times each until you know them well.
Then play the right-hand melodies a few times.

Can you match each chord sequence with the melody that fits the best?
Join your chosen matching pairs with a line.

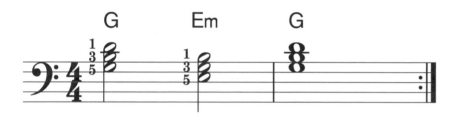

Can you play your matching pairs hands together or with your teacher?

Thingamabobs and Oojamaflips

57/58

G-SHARP (G#) is the BLACK KEY
just to the right of G.

How many can you find on your keyboard?

Accents

An ACCENT above or below a note
tells you to play it louder than the
dynamic marking, so that it stands out.

Accompaniment

Play the left hand only with the student's part. When ready, the student's part should be
played up an octave and the right hand of the accompaniment can be added.

Swung

Eighth Note Rest

The sign ⅞ is an EIGHTH NOTE REST and tells you to be silent for half a count.

Pause

The sign 𝄐 is a PAUSE (or a FERMATA). It tells you to hold the notes marked for longer than their written duration.

The Martian Who Lives in My Fridge

Select a Synth or a Harpsichord voice on your keyboard for this tune.

59/60

Play 4 times then go to ending | ENDING

Count: 1 2 3 and - 4

Accompaniment

Play 4 times | ENDING

Try This

When you have learned the rhythm of this vamp, try adding the third finger in each hand to create these TRIADS:

Cm   Eb   F

C Minor   Eb Major   F Major

61/62

Sports Day

More dynamics

mf stands for MEZZO FORTE (pronounced "met-zoh for-tay"), meaning moderately loud.

mp stands for MEZZO PIANO (pronounced "met-zoh pee-ah-no"), meaning moderately soft.

Accompaniment

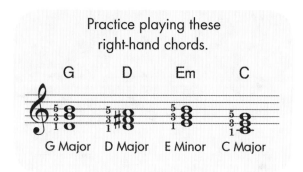

Practice playing these right-hand chords.

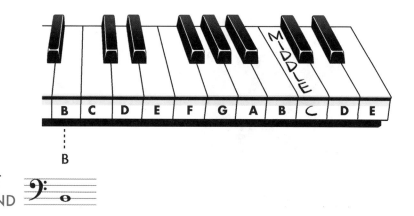

LEFT HAND

The Clifftop Lighthouse

Select a bright Electric Piano or a Grand Piano voice on your keyboard for this tune.

63/64

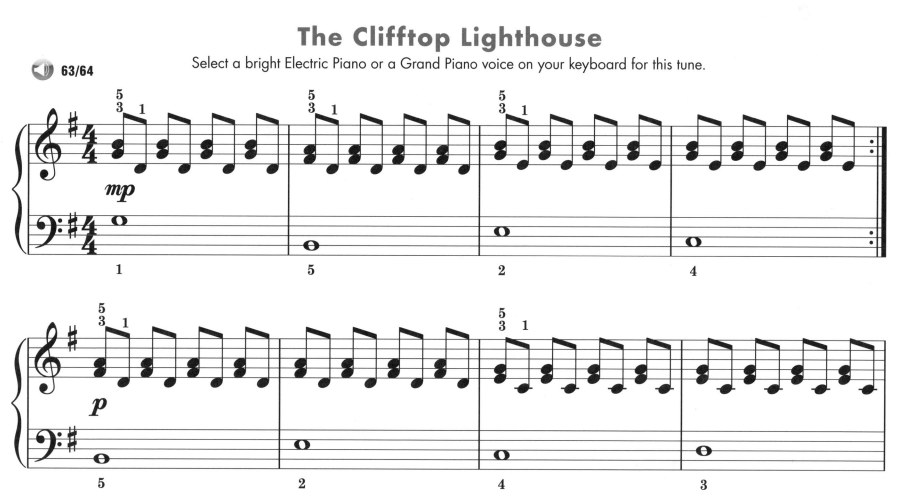

Accompaniment

Certificate of Merit

This certifies that

....

has successfully completed the

EASIEST KEYBOARD COURSE

Teacher

....

Date

....